My
Spiritual
Orgasm

My
Spiritual
Orgasm

Cindy Harris-Saldat

iUniverse, Inc.
Bloomington

My Spiritual Orgasm

iUniverse books may be ordered through booksellers or by contacting:

iUniverse
1663 Liberty Drive
Bloomington, IN 47403
www.iuniverse.com
1-800-Authors (1-800-288-4677)

ISBN: 978-1-4759-7750-9 (sc)
ISBN: 978-1-4759-7752-3 (hc)
ISBN: 978-1-4759-7751-6 (ebk)

Printed in the United States of America

iUniverse rev. date: 02/20/2013

Dedication

Thank you to my dearest daughter, Sarah. Having you gave me the courage and inspiration to get the help I needed for myself in order for you to have the wholesome life you deserve. Your strength, courage and love have made me realize my efforts were well worth my fight. I am so proud of you and love you very much.

To my "sisterhood" who have lifted me up and carried me through moments when I couldn't see the light at the end of the tunnel. I love and cherish you for reaching deep into my spirit when I couldn't find the strength to do so for myself. You made me realize another side of humanity that I was never used to experiencing in my life before.

Thank you all for believing in me and encouraging me to believe in myself.

"Love for everything—want for nothing in return"

Preface

We all endure our own forms of trials and successes. I have been very fortunate to have been given the gift of being able to express mine in writing. From a young age writing was my release. It was a safe place for me to vent and purge my feelings of various emotions and negative points in my life. As my world evolved, writing became my best friend. My writing comes from a lifetime of experience. Growing up in a dysfunctional environment, sexual abuse, toxic relationships, bad choices and chronic illness had brought me to the point where I had lost everything, most importantly, myself. Through therapy and much self-help my journey has allowed me to reach being the person to whom I was intended to be. I now realize that I have been given this special gift in order to utilize it to help others to attain their goal of spiritual freedom.

"We all have a right to feel worthy to live our lives as they were intended for us to be"

Table of Contents

Changes

When you believe, your world opens up

Be glad for yesterday's trials

For it makes us stronger

For a brighter today

And better changes for tomorrow

You have the power within

To make a choice and a change

We learn by changes

And grow by mistakes

With belief all things are possible

And good things don't always have to come to an end

Rely on others

But always count on yourself

Your Passage Through Time

Remembering your smile

Upon entering the room

Your passage through time

Ended much too soon

Your patience and solitude

Your many unspoken words

Your sacrifices and prayers

Have not gone unheard

Embracing the moments

And treasuring the memories

Of a woman who's heart has touched so many

If we had the chance to have known each other

in a different time

Cindy Harris-Saldat

I would have been proud to call you

A good friend of mine

Tears will be of sadness, but of happiness too

That I was blessed for this short time

To have known someone as special as you

God takes his chosen ones for the purpose he has

We may not understand the reason as we leave it in His hands

Such a short span of time but a lifetime filled from above

May eternal peace be with you as you dwell in God's love

Your Higher Power

When you talk

He will listen

When you fall

He will pick you up

When your burdens become too heavy

He knows

You have had enough

When you are happy

He is smiling with you

In your sorrow

He wipes your tears

In your anger

Cindy Harris-Saldat

He calms your spirit

In your terror

He calms your fears

In despair

He holds out His hand

He will pick you up

And carry you

For your life

He has a plan

My Father's Shadow

Fear not

For I am with you

Through the stumbles

And the falls

Although you cannot see me

I am there

Through it all

My hand upon your shoulder

I will guide you

Along the way

I will always be here

Beside you

If you should

Lose your way

I love you beyond measure

In your spirit

I belong

Fear not for I am with you

I will make you strong

Freedom

Give me wings that I may soar

Beyond the very essence of my being

Hold me up that I may not let you down

Let me go higher than I can imagine

For I am ready to evolve

Into the person I need to be

Take flight and be free

From all that binds me

Give me wisdom

That I know the heights I can achieve

For this shall be me

And no other can hold me from that

For my dreams are my destiny

Cindy Harris-Saldat

My Father

A man of few words

But words to live by

Driven by loyalty to life and land

Surviving so much

Yet having unspoken compassion

A survivor at his best

In his silence I felt his strength

In his anger I felt his power

In his persistence I saw his courage

In his face I saw his pain

In his spirit I knew his lonliness

As his strength weakened and his anger diminished

His soul ached to be free from pain

With frustration ravaging him he fought to the end

It was then the angels rescued him

Rewarding him with eternal peace

Now in my silence I feel his strength

In my anger I feel his power

In my face I see his pain

In my spirit I feel his lonliness

So I know he will be with me forever

Cindy Harris-Saldat

I'll Be With You

You will hear me in the silence

You will see me in your dreams

You will feel my love surround you

For I am many things

I will be the flowers in your garden

The breeze upon your face

I will be the trees swaying

For I am in a different place

I'll be the silent footsteps

That lead you where you go

I'll be the voice within you

For I love you so

My Spiritual Orgasm

Close your eyes and imagine yourself on a beautiful beach

Cool white sand between your toes

The warmth of the sun enveloping you like nature's blanket

The sound of the waves hypnotizing your thoughts

The gentle breeze caressing every pore

Your thoughts seem to float away

You are at total peace

The life that was intended for you to feel

Suddenly without warning you feel a chill

Opening your eyes, you see the clouds overtaking the sun

The shadows on the sand are unwelcoming

The breeze has now become stronger,

sending a chill down your spine

It picks up the grains of sand and tosses them about

You can feel them against your skin like needles from a pine tree

The sound of the waves has become harsh and rapid

Like the beating of your heart

As fast as it's approach it dissipates

The sun comes out and warms you as a slight breeze blows past

The crashing of the waves surrender

As the darkness has now passed

A new spark is born

Puzzles

Our lives are like puzzles

Some are complete, some are not

Some have many pieces, some hardly any at all

Some of us it will take longer

To complete our puzzle task

Some of us will figure it out quickly and be able to do it fast

Some pieces have many colors, some very few

Either way we must use our senses and put in lots of thought

To complete the puzzle properly because every piece has it's spot

If you are finding your puzzle you cannot complete

Maybe some pieces are missing or broken

Cindy Harris-Saldat

And it's becoming a real feat

Don't despair, there's always a way to finish

You may have to create your own pieces

and practice to make them fit

It may be simple or take more work

It may be frustrating, it's true

In the end you can stand back proudly

and look at it and smile

And wonder why you worried so much

When you were doing it all the while

Renewal

Quiet and calming

Intensifying every smell

Close your eyes

Breathe deep

Relax your mind

Let your body go limp

For at this moment

There is no pain

No sorrow

Focus on your heart

Listen to it beating

Constant and rhythmic

Feel your body become whole

Your breathing is deep

Cleansing your mind

As you become one with yourself

Your spirit is renewed

Miracles

Once in a while

A miracle will happen

Right before your eyes

And if you are lucky enough

You will come to realize

That all things happen for a reason

And all things come in time

If you allow yourself to believe in that

The peace that comes from honoring it

Will remain with you for all time

Homemade Self Esteem Stew

2 cups of confidence

Pinch of self-assurance

1 cup self-love

2 tablespoons ego

1 cup boundaries

1 pound good choices

Season with happiness and fun

Mix all ingredients together well in a large pot.

Bring to a gentle simmer. The longer you leave it to simmer

the better it turns out. Serve with Guilt-Free Dumplings

GUILT-FREE DUMPLINGS

1 tablespoon crushed anger

1 cup worry-free crackers, finely crushed

2 tablespoons control

1 pkg. inner beauty

1 tablespoon success

Place worry-free crackers in a large mixing bowl.

Slowly add crushed anger until completely dissolved. Mix well.

Gently stir in inner beauty, just until blended, being careful

not to overmix. Divide into equal sized spoonfuls

and drop gently and evenly over stew.

NOTE: This stew is very fulfilling and can also be served

with an order of Chips Off Your Shoulder

Cindy Harris-Saldat

Example

E—e

X—xtra

A—accompaniment of

M—my

P—personal

L—life

E—experiences

For Example:

My 3 L's . . . LOVE, LESSONS AND LAUGHTER

LOVE: love of self and love from others will support you

in life's journey

LESSONS: lessons learned . . . whether past,

present or future will provide you with the knowledge

you will need on your journey

LAUGHTER: being able to laugh at yourself

and laugh along with others will make your emotional journey

a much more pleasant one!

Cindy Harris-Saldat

Quotes For Your Day

Count your blessings every day . . .

no matter how small they may seem

Blessings are like bonuses . . . don't expect them . . .

just be grateful for them

Life is granted to us . . . not that we should take it for such

Make today's choices wisely . . .

as tomorrow will be a reflection of them

Peace within comes from your body,

mind and spirit coming together in perfect harmony

Let your hands do the work of your heart, your body flow

in rythmn to your spirit and your voice echo your thoughts

The measure of accomplishment is not how long it takes you

to climb a mountain but rather the strategy

you use to get to the top

Being in love with the passion of helping others

is different than from others being in love with the passion

of helping themselves

Life is not based on the ability to reflect on the past but rather

to look to the future . . . who, what or where you have been

is not important . . . who, what and where you are now is

Finding your inner beauty is like working

on an archeological dig . . . once you brush away

all the dirt the real treasure is underneath

Let me bathe in the beauty of simple pleasures

Wealth does not validate a person

nor should it dictate one's standards

Fulfilled are those who know where contentment lies

Like a tree reaches out it's branches toward the sky in growth

so does my soul in search for acceptance within

My soul is my gateway to my spirit and my spirit is my destiny

Motivate

M—Move

O—On

T—To

I—Initiate

V—Various

A—Activities

T—Through

E—Everyday life

Motivate yourself to get up and get moving

Initiate . . . don't wait for others to be your guide

Enjoy your life through various activities you enjoy . . . or try

something new and daring . . . challenge yourself!

"May the breeze blow away the clutter and the sunshine

light your path"

Remember

When your head is heavy

And your shoulders can bear no more

When the ache in your soul is relentless

Remember, I too have been there before

When your tears will not subside

And the darkness is closing in

When your self esteem seems shattered

Remember where I have been

When you feel all hope is lost

And life seems a living hell

When you shut out all the world

Remember, into the same depths I fell

But life can change in a moment

Depending on which path you take

I chose the one less travelled

And did it for my own sake

It took time, patience and perseverance

And was bumpy along the way

But my life has taken on new meaning

And I am grateful for every day

Your Gift

Everyone possesses one

Everyone's is unique

You will recognize it

If you see it

Treasure it

Utilize it

But handle it with care

It is a privilege not a right

It will be a part of your life

And lives to come

Be thankful for it everyday

Sometimes it can be well hidden

Allow yourself to dream

And you will find it

It is your gift

Cindy Harris-Saldat

Serenity

Remember your child's eyes are a reflection of you

Cherish your pets

Don't take anything for granted

Love yourself . . . be grateful for every breath

Value your surroundings and enjoy your friends

Never leave on a bad note for tomorrow may not come

If you raise your voice—don't raise your hand

Keep memories close to your heart

Meditate . . . take time for you

Know your boundaries

Step up when you're wrong

Don't be afraid to be yourself

Listen to others . . . you may learn something

Take each day as it comes and appreciate what each day holds

Help those less fortunate . . . even if it's your time you can afford

Try not to be hurtful to others or yourself

When you lay your head on your pillow at night be thankful

for your blessings and obstacles

Each one is put in your path for a reason

Allow yourself all these experiences

and when you close your eyes to enter into sleep

It will be a peaceful one

Friends

If all of you were flowers

I would plant you in a row

In a garden of many colors

To the world I would show

That each and every one of you

Is a blessing from above

You are filled with caring and thoughtfulness

And unconditional love

Never will I forget

All that you have done

For getting me through the hard times

I thank you, each and every one

My heart cannot express

The emotion you have made me feel

At times when life is lowest and things seem so surreal

All the acts of kindness that you all have shown

And all the gifts you've shared

I can now lay my head on my pillow at night

And be thankful someone cared

I don't know what I have done

to deserve such friends as you

I just hope someday I can repay the debt

and be there for all of you

Cindy Harris-Saldat

Layered Dysfunctional Salad

3 cups control

1 cup shame

1 cup quiet

2 cups verbal abuse

2 cups emotional abuse

2 cups physical abuse

Pinch of sexual abuse

2 tablespoons real tears

1 cup emptiness

5 tablespoons depression

2 teaspoons confusion

This salad has no specific way in which it is layered.

You can also, change the quantities of each ingredient

as needed, depending on how you feel that day.

It can be topped off with any of the dressings below.

Disconnected Dressing

No Value Dressing

Failure Dressing

Mixture of Hate and Codependency(be sure to shake well first)

NOTE: some of these ingredients can be substituted for similar

dysfunctional ones. It doesn't matter if the quantities of each

ingredient are off a bit . . . the end result will be the same.

At The End

Allow yourself to smile

Allow yourself to cry

And when the end draws near

Allow yourself to say goodbye

For it through you and about you

That love will shine it's rays

In your absence

All will give praise

Like a rainbow shines after a storm

It's beauty offers peace and tranquility

So shall it be

For your disheartened soul

Creation

When you look around at your surroundings

At the world created for us

It is hard to imagine

All was done by God's touch

Every blade of grass . . . every flower

Every cloud and ray of sun

Every animal

Every whisper and every sound

The seas and lakes

The waterfalls and ponds

Cindy Harris-Saldat

Every fish . . . every creature

Every plant, bird and bug

All the people of different origin

God created in His love

For this we all must cherish

We are only here but once

A pit stop on our journey

To eternal peace and love

Time

Time is a gift

That goes by too fast

Being grateful for now

Can be the hardest task

When life is at it's lowest

And all hope seems to be lost

Remember only one thing

That time is the cost

We can't bring it back

Nor predict when it will end

So enjoy it daily

Use it wisely, my friend

Cindy Harris-Saldat

Believe

Blessed are those who believe

That love can conquer all

Through our failings

There is new found wisdom

Through our faith, new beginnings

Through our courage comes strength

Through our trying times, new hope

Through our patience comes endless possiblilities

Through our love our spirit soars

For without love

Even in it's simplicity

The world becomes bleak

Reach out to others

But above all

Reach out to yourself

Let your surroundings be your guide

Encircle yourself with like minds

And peace and serenity will be yours

Cindy Harris-Saldat

As Night Falls

There is a place in my heart

Where it feels it has been torn apart

All my wishes

All my dreams

Have somehow faded

Forever it seems

Silent pictures in my mind

Of a place I have left behind

Broken promises that have been made

In my sleep I see them fade

As tears stream down upon my face

There is so much too hard to erase

And so I pray my God above

Will grant me happiness, health and love

For my faith will guide me through

When I feel there is nothing more than I can do

Believe in me and trust in Him

And there rests a smile upon my face

As I thank Him for all His grace

As night falls and I lay down

My mind is peaceful without a sound

Cindy Harris-Saldat

Anorexia Of The Soul

If the human body can be starved

So can the soul

Consciencely or unconsciencely

The soul can be depleted from it's very existence

Starved and weak

It becomes unable to perform it's task

As fuel diminishes . . . so does it's light

As your body strives for the nourishment it needs

So does your soul to survive

Rightfully Mine

What was taken from me

Was rightfully mine

Not measured materially

But measured in time

What began as pure was marred by disgust

For that reason . . . I had lost all trust

Full of bad choices and many regrets

Memories are tarnished but lest I forget

I cannot change the past

The future I embrace

Shadows of lost time

I can only erase

The conscience minds of those

That crossed that line

Will never forget

What was rightfully mine

The Trickle Of Water

The trickle of water

Gently winding through the pebbles

Choosing it's path

Slowly nudging it's way over rocks

Gaining momentum and strength

With speed and perseverance

Pushing it's way forward

Raw energy cascading over obstacles in it's path

Broken and disguarded

Cindy Harris-Saldat

Turbulent and angry

Circling in all directions

It's wrath becomes exhausted and spent

A calm existence now

A steady flow

A balance of nature

It unites into a partnership of larger proportion

A journey to the innermost depths of it's soul

Thank You

To the ones who gave me life

Thank you

To the ones who betrayed me

Thank you . . . they were lessons well taught

To the ones that took advantage

Thank you . . . now your conscience is your guide

To the ones who filled me with laughter

Thank you for my smile

To the ones who gave me opportunity

Thank you for believing in me

To my daughter

Thank you for your love and understanding

To the ones who taught me to love myself

Thank you for your patience

To the ones who stood by me

Thank you for not leaving

To all those who enriched my life

Whether by hardships or love

Thank you for helping me understand my value

In Silence

In silence I will walk with you

I will hold your hand

Though you won't feel it

I will kiss your face

Though there will be no touch

I will hold you close

Though my presence cannot be seen

I will be your voice within

Cindy Harris-Saldat

When you don't know where to turn

I will sit next to you

When you are lonely

I will never abandon you

For I love you

I will be with you forever

I will be waiting for you

When you need me most

I Surrender

I surrender my weakness

So that I can be strong

I surrender my failings

For all I've done wrong

I surrender my confusion

So my path may become clear

I surrender my anxiety

Cindy Harris-Saldat

So there will be no more fear

The power within me

That comes from above

Shows me the signs

Of unconditional love

All things within reason

All things in good time

With belief and patience

Good things can be mine

Lend Me

Lend me your mind, I will give it wisdom

Lend me your eyes, I will show them beauty

Lend me your ears, you will hear the sound of angels

Lend me your voice, I will give it knowledge

Lend me your shoulders, I will lift your burdens

Lend me your hands, I will give them work

Lend me your feet, I will show them direction

Lend me your heart, I will give it love

Lend me your soul, I will give it purpose

Lend me your spirit, I will give it peace

Lend me your pain, I will show it justice

Lend me your fears, I will give them rest

Lend me your life, I will make it whole

Cindy Harris-Saldat

The Four Seasons Of Life

Spring is a time of renewal

A time for growth

Summer is a time to nurture

Providing nourishment to the soul

Autumn is a time for preparation

A time for cleaning out the clutter in our lives

Winter is a time to take inventory

Of things we need to survive

Life's Lessons

We are all handed lessons in life

Whether they be easy or hard

We take each one and do with it

What will eventually make us proud

The easy ones don't take much time

And are simpler to solve

The harder ones are more difficult

Sometimes seeming there is no resolve

No matter how they come to you

Whether person, place or thought

As long as you have solved them

There will be an end result

Of challenges and compromise

Consequences and pain

What may seem darkest at that moment

Is put in place for a reason

So eventually peace will reign

He Is Always There

He has created a world for us

He is our parent, our teacher, our friend

Our confidant, our provider, our keeper

In our darkness He brings us light

In the shadows He watches over us

In our despair He holds our heart near

In our joy He celebrates with us

In our anger He calms us

Cindy Harris-Saldat

In our silence He listens

In our hopes He hears

In our lonliness He comforts us

In our loss He consoles us

In our peace He rejoices with us

In our death

He is one with us

The Meeting Place

There is a special meeting place

Waiting for me somewhere

Where my body, mind and spirit

Will be getting together to share

I am finding it rather difficult though

For us all to meet at once

Either my body is busy, my mind is away

or my spirit is gone for months

But it is very important to do this

because time is ticking away

And the longer it is left the wider the gap

And from each other we will stray

At times I can go without connecting

but the day does finally come

When I feel an emptiness inside,

second guessing the person I've become

So you see it is very crucial to it is necessary

to get with them as soon as I can

And stay on track of how we are each doing

and areas we need to mend

It is necessary to work on this together

For we each play an important role

If one of us is lacking, on all it takes it's toll

So our meeting place has to be decided

And joining up is a must

For ultimately we are all one

And in each other we believe and trust

Cindy Harris-Saldat

That Was You

A whisper

A breath in my ear

A voice in my head

A memory in my heart

My soul awakens

My spirit soars

To a familiar place

A song

A tear

A smile

A faint murmur

A trace of what was

A gift

That was you

Taking Chances

Mighty are those who persevere

Never to turn back

Not denying fate

But embracing new beginnings

Savouring life's pleasures

Following destiny's path

Taking chances and risking all

Believing that the path they take

Will fulfill their journey

And accepting the peace it holds

Cindy Harris-Saldat

Internal Fertilizer

It is said you reap what you sow

If you sow bad seed

Your crop will not develop to it's full capacity

If you do not fertilize it

It will not grow to it's abundance

It is like your body, mind and soul

Your spirit needs a good start internally

to be able to know it's direction

Seeds are sown invisibly under the earth

With the proper nourishment

and care they will break through the soil

Beginning their journey to maturity

Checking on them and seeing if they require

additional attention is beneficial

Some thrive better in the shade . . . some in the sun

Some in drier areas . . . some in moist

All are unique and have different needs

All need the basic necessities in order to grow

Just like the seeds

We all have basic needs

We all have unique requirements

We all thrive in different areas

Some need more care and attention to reach our goal

Cindy Harris-Saldat

Bio

Cindy Harris-Saldat grew up in Winona, Ontario, Canada.
She works in the healthcare field and currently resides
with her daughter, Sarah and her two dogs in Hamilton,
Ontario, Canada